COOL
MAKERSPACE

GADGETS & GIZMOS

LIGHT IT!

CREATIONS THAT GLOW, SHINE, AND BLINK

Christa Schneider

Checkerboard
Library

An Imprint of Abdo Publishing
abdopublishing.com

abdopublishing.com

Printed in the United States of America, North Mankato, Minnesota
102017
012018

THIS BOOK CONTAINS
RECYCLED MATERIALS

Design: Sarah DeYoung, Mighty Media, Inc.
Production: Mighty Media, Inc.
Editor: Liz Salzmann
Cover Photographs: Mighty Media, Inc.; Shutterstock
Interior Photographs: iStockphoto; Mighty Media, Inc.; Shutterstock

The following manufacturers/names appearing in this book are trademarks: Alltrade®, Duracell®, Elmer's®, Energizer®, LEGO®, littleBits™, Mod Podge®, Rapala®

Publisher's Cataloging-in-Publication Data
Names: Schneider, Christa, author.
Title: Light it! creations that glow, shine, and blink / by Christa
    Schneider.
Other titles: Creations that glow, shine, and blink
Description: Minneapolis, Minnesota : Abdo Publishing, 2018. |
    Series: Cool makerspace gadgets & gizmos | Includes online
    resources and index.
Identifiers: LCCN 2017944033 | ISBN 9781532112539 (lib.bdg.) |
    ISBN 9781614799955 (ebook)
Subjects: LCSH: Electronics--Juvenile literature. | Creative ability
    in science--Juvenile literature. | Handicraft--Juvenile literature. |
    Makerspaces--Juvenile literature.
Classification: DDC 621.381--dc23
LC record available at https://lccn.loc.gov/2017944033

TO ADULT HELPERS

This is your chance to assist a young maker as they develop new skills, gain confidence, and make cool things! These activities are designed to help children create projects in makerspaces. Children may need more assistance for some activities than others. Be there to offer guidance when they need it. Encourage them to do as much as they can on their own. Be a cheerleader for their creativity.

Before getting started, remember to lay down ground rules for using tools and supplies and for cleaning up. There should always be adult supervision when using a hot or sharp tool.

SAFETY SYMBOLS

Some projects in this book require the use of hot or sharp tools. That means you'll need some adult help for these projects. Determine whether you'll need help on a project by looking for these safety symbols.

HOT!
This project requires the use of a hot tool.

SHARP!
This project requires the use of a sharp tool.

CONTENTS

What's a MAKERSPACE?

Picture a place bursting with creativity. In every direction, you see designers and light artists building amazing projects that glow, shine, and blink. Welcome to a makerspace!

Makerspaces are areas where people come together to create. They are the perfect places to design and create light projects! Makerspaces have all kinds of materials and tools. But a maker's best tool is his or her imagination. Makers think of new light projects. They also find ways to improve existing light projects. Then, they bring these creations to life! Are you ready to become a maker?

BEFORE YOU GET STARTED

GET PERMISSION

Ask an adult for **permission** to use the makerspace and materials before starting any project.

BE RESPECTFUL

Share tools and supplies with other makers. When you're done with a tool, put it back so others can use it.

MAKE A PLAN

Read through the instructions and gather all your supplies ahead of time. Keep them organized as you create!

BE SAFE

Working with electricity can be **dangerous**, so be careful! Keep your power source switched off when connecting wires. Prevent short circuits. Ask an adult for help when you need it.

WHAT CREATES LIGHT?

Light can be natural or artificial. Natural light comes from the sun. It is what allows us to see the world around us. Fire is another kind of natural light. For thousands of years, people used fire to see at night and in dark places.

In the 1800s, scientists figured out how to use electricity to create artificial light. Today, there are many types of light bulbs that can be lit with electric circuits. Many of them work great for lighting up all kinds of maker projects.

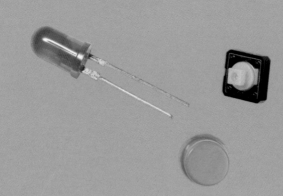

LED LIGHTS

Light Emitting Diodes (LEDs) are small light bulbs with wires. When you connect the wires in an electric circuit, the bulb lights up! LEDs come in many colors and can be used in different ways to light up your maker projects.

LITTLEBITS

littleBits is a brand of electronic building blocks. Types of littleBits parts include motors, power sources, and light wire. The pieces are magnetic, so they're easy to fit together. These pieces can be used to make many electronic inventions. Then you can take your invention apart and use the pieces to make something new!

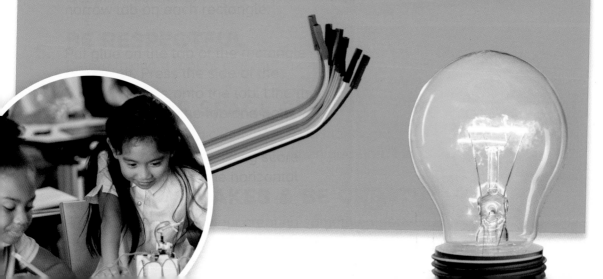

SUPPLIES

Here are some of the materials and tools used for the projects in this book. If your makerspace doesn't have these supplies, don't worry! Good makers are good problem solvers. Find different supplies to substitute for your missing materials. Modify the projects to make them your own. Be creative!

cardboard box
with flaps

craft knife

duct tape

fishing line

glue stick

hot glue gun
& glue sticks

LED light
string

LEDs

LEGO basic
bricks

LEGO bushings
for cross axles

LEGO cross
axles

LEGO double
conical
wheels

littleBits
Gizmos &
Gadgets Kit

littleBits
light wire

8

LIGHT IT! TECHNIQUES

Mod Podge

needle-nose
pliers

9-volt
battery

3-volt button
battery

DESIGN AND FUNCTION TIP

It's okay to make mistakes when building light-up **gadgets** and gizmos. Many of the materials and parts can be taken apart and reused. If a part that should light up doesn't, check all the wire connections. And if you're not happy with the way something works or looks, just try again!

STRIPPING WIRES

A light needs an electric circuit to work. Circuits are made with wire and a power source. Wire often comes coated in plastic **insulation**. To make a connection, the insulation has to be stripped off the end of the wire. A wire stripper makes this easy. Place the wire stripper over the wire near the end. Gently squeeze the wire stripper's handles while moving the tool toward the end of the wire. Don't squeeze too hard, or you will cut the wire! And don't try to strip too much insulation at once. Strip the wire in small sections.

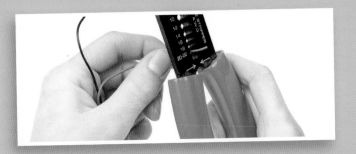

GLOW MASK

Make a fun, futuristic mask with functioning lights!

10

1. Draw a mask shape on a piece of cardboard. Make the mask 19 inches long by 7 inches wide (48 by 18 cm).

2. In the center of the bottom of the mask, draw an upside-down *V*. This is the section of the mask that will sit on your nose once it is cut out.

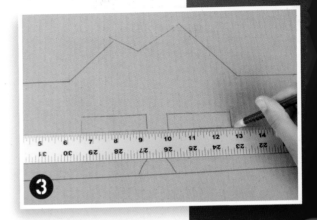

3. Draw two rectangles above the nose cutout for eye holes.

4. Cut the outer edges of the mask out.

5. Make marks 6 inches (15 cm) in from each side of the mask. Use the ruler and craft knife to lightly **score** a vertical line at each mark. This will allow you to fold the sides of the mask to make **temples**.

6. Carefully use a craft knife to cut out the eye holes.

7. Cover your work surface with newspaper. Paint the mask. Let the paint dry.

Continued on the next page.

8 Fold the sides of the mask back at the **score** lines. Put duct tape along the folds. Tuck the duct tape into the folds so the **temples** can fully bend back.

9. Put duct tape over all the edges of the mask.

10. Plan the path for the light wire. It can go all around the mask, but should end at an edge of the mask. This is so you can hide the wires behind the mask.

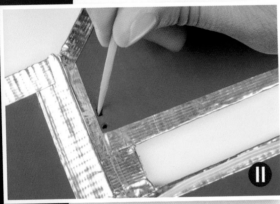

11 Use a toothpick to make two holes at each spot where you want the light wire to turn. The two holes in each pair should be ¼ inch (0.6 cm) apart.

12. Cut a piece of thin wire for each pair of holes. Make each piece about 2 inches (5 cm) long.

13 Lay the light wire along the path. Start with the end that doesn't have the connector. At each pair of holes, stick the ends of a thin wire through the holes over the light wire. Twist the ends of the thin wire together behind the mask.

14 After the light wire is fully attached, turn the mask over. Cover the twisted wire ends with duct tape. This will keep them from poking you when you wear the mask.

15. Tape the unattached part of the light wire inside one of the **temples**. It should hang down past the bottom of the mask.

16. Hold the mask over your face and fold the temples back. Have someone measure the distance between the ends of the temples. Cut a piece of elastic string as long as the measurement.

17 Staple an end of the elastic string to the inside of each temple. Try the mask on. Adjust the string if necessary.

18 Connect the 9-volt battery to the power bit. Then connect the power bit to the light wire bit.

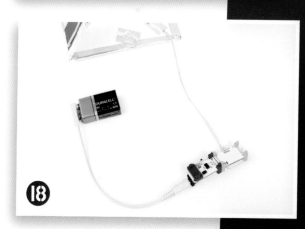

19. Put the mask on. Turn on the power switch to light it up! Hide the power assembly in a shirt pocket or under a scarf.

SPARKLEBALL

Construct a glowing globe to add sparkle to any room!

1. Cover your work surface with newspaper. Hot glue the sides of the cups together until they form a circle. This should take about 11 or 12 cups.

2. Make a second layer of cups by hot gluing more cups to the cups in the first layer. This should take about nine cups. Add additional glue between the cups in the second layer to keep them secure.

3. Make the third layer of cups by hot gluing more cups to the cups in the second layer. This should take about three or four cups. Add additional glue between cups if necessary. The cups should now form a **dome** shape.

4. Repeat steps 1 through 3 to create a second dome. Let the glue dry.

Continued on the next page.

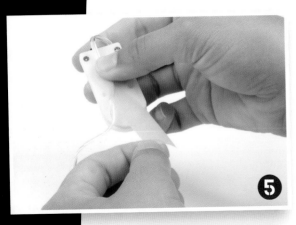

5 Put a piece of tape on the edge of the LED light string switch.

6 Turn one of the **domes** over. Put the switch between two cups. Make sure it points toward the outside of the dome. Tape the switch to a cup. Add more tape if necessary to secure it.

7 Cut piece of fishing line about 5 feet (1.5 m) long. Thread the ends of the fishing line through the dome between the cups near the switch. Tie the ends of the line in a knot.

8 Pull the line to the outside of the **dome**. Glue the knot to the bottom of a cup to help secure it.

9 Loosely bundle the LED light string inside the dome.

10. Place the second dome on the first dome to create a **sphere**. Shift the domes around until the cups fit together well.

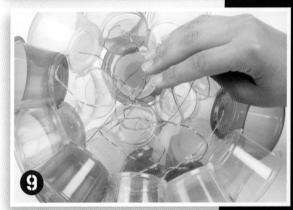

11 Once you find the right position, have a friend hold the domes in place. Glue the domes together. Put glue where cups from each dome meet. Let the glue dry.

12. Use the fishing line to hang up your sparkleball. Turn the switch on to see it glow!

UFO

Build a blinking, spinning
spacecraft!

WHAT YOU NEED

littleBits Gizmos & Gadgets Kit parts (power bit, DC motor, motorMate,
2 BLE bits, split bit)

LEGOs (2 20-tooth double conical wheels, 3M cross axle,
basic bricks, 2×6 plate with holes, bushing for cross axle, 5M cross axle,
8-tooth double conical wheel)

large rubber band • 9-volt battery • adhesive foam

2 aluminum foil pie tins • craft knife • cutting mat

hot glue gun & glue sticks • small hook-and-loop dot

1. Connect the power bit to the DC motor bit. It doesn't matter which direction the motor is set on.

2 Put the motorMate on the motor shaft. Put a 20-tooth double conical wheel on the 3M cross **axle**. Stick the axle into the other end of the motorMate.

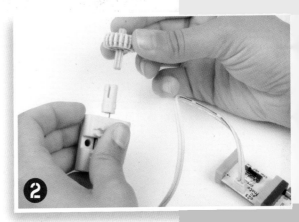

3. Build a base out of LEGOs. It should have a place for the motor to sit with the shaft pointing up. Build a tower on each side that is higher than the 20-tooth double conical wheel. There should also be a space for the motor's wire to come out.

4 Set the DC motor on the base.

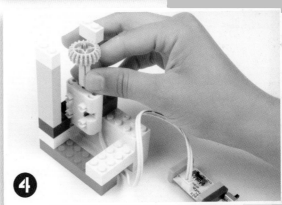

5. Wrap a rubber band around the motor and one tower.

6 Twist the rubber band and wrap it around the motor and both towers.

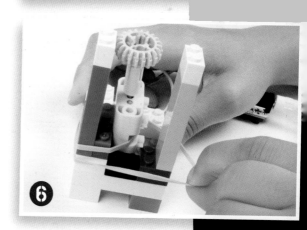

Continued on the next page.

7. Pull the second loop of the rubber band out. Set the battery inside the rubber band. The positive side of the battery should be next to the LEGO tower.

8 Connect the power bit's wire to the battery.

9 Place the 2×6 plate with holes on top of the towers. Make sure the LEGO piece doesn't touch the wheel.

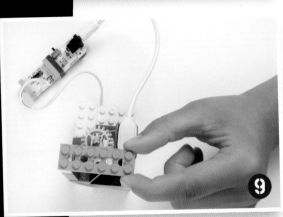

10. Put the bushing and the second 20-tooth double conical wheel onto the 5M cross **axle**. Adjust the bushing to keep the wheel at the end of the axle.

11 Stick the other end of the 5M cross axle through the center hole of the 2×6 plate. Put the 8-tooth double conical wheel on the end. Make sure the teeth of the small wheel **interlock** with the teeth of the large wheel on the motor shaft.

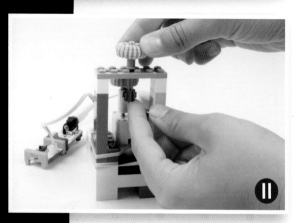

12. Attach a BLE bit to each of the two separate ends of the split bit.

⑬ Connect the split bit to the motor bit opposite from the power bit.

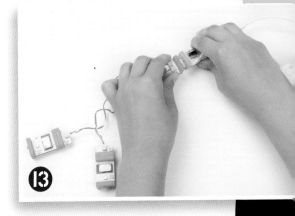

⑭ Use **adhesive foam** to stick the BLE bits to the towers. Tape the wires to the base too.

⑮ Carefully use the craft knife to cut rectangles out of the sides of the pie tins. Cut a circle out of the bottom of one pie tin. Make sure the hole fits over your entire LEGO structure.

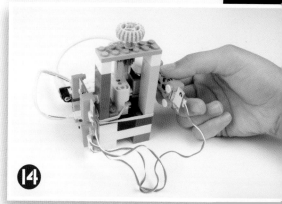

16. Put hot glue around the rim of one pie tin. Turn the second pie tin over. Place it on top of the first pie tin to form a UFO shape. Let the glue dry.

17. Set the UFO down with the round hole facing up. Stick one side of the hook-and-loop dot inside the UFO. Center it in the bottom tin. Stick the other side of the hook-and-loop dot to the top of the upper large wheel.

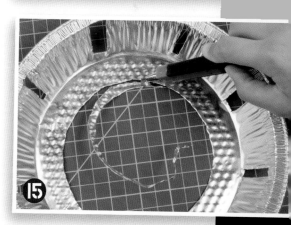

18. Turn the UFO over and set it on the base. Press the sides of the hook-and-loop dot together.

19. Switch the motor on. Watch your UFO spin and light up!

TOUCH LAMP

Amaze your friends with this magical looking lamp!

WHAT YOU NEED

small tin with a clear lid • duct tape

hammer • nail • colored tissue paper

Mod Podge • small paintbrush • wire cutter

insulated wire • wire stripper • 2 LEDs

needle-nose pliers • electrical tape

3-volt button battery

aluminum foil

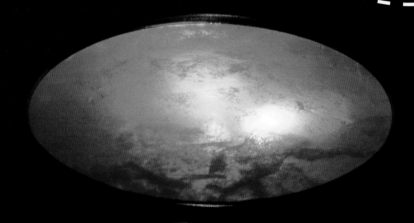

I. Remove the tin's lid. Line the inside of the tin with duct tape. This will keep the metal from interfering with the electric circuit.

2 Turn the tin over. Carefully hammer a nail through the bottom of the tin.

3. Tear small pieces of tissue paper. Paint the inside of the lid with Mod Podge. Press the tissue paper pieces into the Mod Podge. Keep adding tissue paper until the clear part of the lid is covered. Let it dry.

4 Cut two 3-inch (7.5 cm) pieces of electrical wire. These are the long wires. Cut another piece of wire that is 2 inches (2.5 cm) long. This is the short wire. Strip both ends of the three wires. See page 9 for a tip on how to strip a wire.

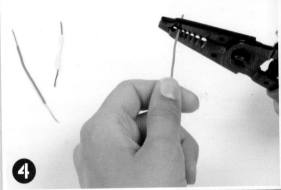

5 Use pliers to twist the longer leads of both LEDs and one end of a long wire together. Then twist the short leads of both LEDs and one end of the other long wire together.

Continued on the next page.

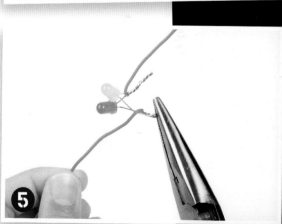

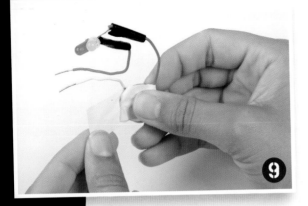

6. Put electrical tape over each pair of twisted wire and leads.

7. Bend the loose end of each long wire into a small loop. Hold one loop to one side of the battery. Hold the other loop to the other side of the battery. If the LEDs don't light up, try switching the loops.

8. When the LEDs light up, tape one of the loops to the battery. Let the other loop go to disconnect the circuit.

9 Twist one end of the short wire into a loop. Hold the loop to the side of the battery opposite from the taped long wire. Tape the loop in place.

10. Push the two loose wire ends through the hole in the tin from the inside. Pull them through until the stripped parts of each end are completely outside the tin.

11 Center the LEDs inside the tin. Arrange the excess wire lengths neatly around the LEDs. Tape the wires in place inside the tin.

12 Turn the tin over. Fold small pieces of foil around the end of each wire. The pieces of foil should form rectangles.

13 Arrange the two rectangles so one hovers over the other, but the two rectangles are not touching.

14. Put the lid on the tin. Press the rectangles together against the bottom of the tin. Watch your lamp light up!

SPINNING
NEBULA

Simulate a supersize wonder of
the galaxy in a small box!

1. Cut pieces of white card stock to fit in the bottom and along each side of the box. Glue the pieces in place.

2. Set the box down with the short sides on the left and right. Cut the right-hand flap 1 inch (2.5 cm) from the crease.

3. Tip the box on its side. Place the glass tile on the edge of the flap that is resting on the table. Trace around the tile. Cut slightly inside the lines.

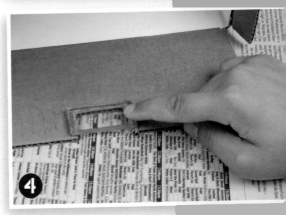

4. Cover your work surface with newspaper. Hot glue the glass tile over the cut-out rectangle. Let the glue dry.

5. Draw a 1½-inch (4 cm) circle on the box's top flap. It should be 1 inch (2.5 cm) in from the flap's right and top edges. Cut out the circle.

6. Cut a piece of fishing line 6 inches (15 cm) long. Hot glue one end of the line to the edge of the glass pebble. Let the glue dry.

Continued on the next page.

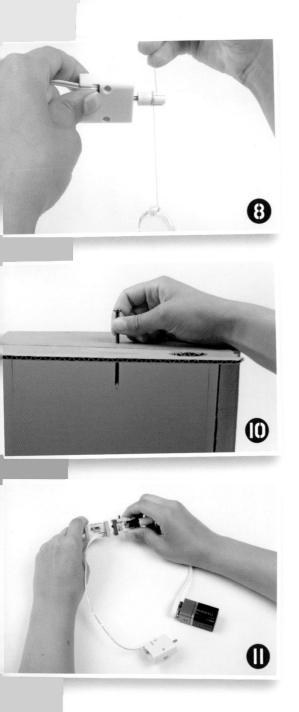

7. Close the box's bottom flap. Measure from the top of the rectangular glass tile to the top of the box. Subtract ½ inch (1.25 cm). Use a permanent marker to mark the fishing line that distance from the pebble.

8 Put the motorMate on the motor shaft. Thread the loose end of the fishing line through the end of the motorMate. Pull it through until the mark on the line is just below the motorMate. Wrap the line around the motorMate and through the slots several times.

9. Tape the fishing line to the motorMate with duct tape. Trim the extra line. Remove the motorMate from the motor.

10 Set the glass pebble on top of the box ½ inch (1.25 cm) from the flap. Make sure it's centered between both ends of the box. Mark the box under the center of the pebble. Poke a nail through the mark. Wiggle the nail around to widen the hole.

11 Connect the battery to the power bit. Connect the power bit to the motor.

12 Set the motor on the box with the shaft through the hole you made it step 10. Connect the motorMate to the motor shaft inside the box. Secure the parts to the top of the box with duct tape.

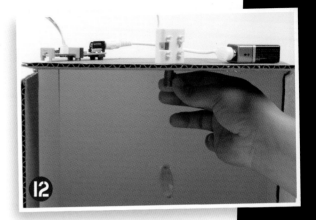

13. Close the box flaps and tape them shut. Do not tape over the round hole or the glass tile.

14 Connect the wire bit to the BLE bit. Connect the other end of the wire bit to the motor.

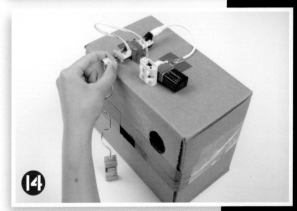

15. Tape the BLE bit over the rectangular tile so that the light shines through the tile.

16. Turn the motor on and look through the round hole. You'll be amazed by the **stellar**, spinning light show!

MAKERSPACE MAINTENANCE

Being a maker is not just about the finished craft. It's about communicating and **collaborating** with others as you create. The best makers also learn from their creations. They think of ways to improve them next time.

CLEANING UP

When you're done with a project, be sure to tidy up your area. Put away tools and supplies. Make sure they are organized so others can find them easily.

SAFE STORAGE

Sometimes you won't finish a project in one makerspace **session**. That's OK! Just find a safe place to store your project until you can work on it again.

MAKER FOR LIFE!

Maker project possibilities are endless. Get inspired by the materials in your makerspace. Invite new makers to your space. Check out what other makers are creating. Never stop making!

GLOSSARY

adhesive foam – craft foam that has one or more sticky sides.

axle – a bar that connects two wheels.

collaborate – to work with another person or group in order to do something or reach a goal.

dangerous – able or likely to cause harm or injury.

dome – a rounded top or roof that looks like half of a ball.

gadget – a tool or device that does a specific job or task.

insulation – material used to keep something from losing or transferring electricity, heat, or sound.

interlock – to attach by putting one part inside another.

permission – when a person in charge says it's okay to do something.

score – to mark with a line or scratch.

session – a period of time used for a specific purpose or activity.

sphere – a solid figure that is round, such as a ball or a globe, and has every point the same distance from the center.

stellar – related to the stars.

temple – one of the side parts of a pair of glasses that rest on the ears.

ONLINE RESOURCES

Booklinks
NONFICTION
NETWORK
FREE! ONLINE NONFICTION RESOURCES

To learn more about projects that light up, visit **abdobooklinks.com**. These links are routinely monitored and updated to provide the most current information available.

INDEX